# A NOTE TO PARENTS

When your children are ready to "step into reading," giving them the right books—and lots of them—is as crucial as giving them the right food to eat. **Step into Reading Books** present exciting stories and information reinforced with lively, colorful illustrations that make learning to read fun, satisfying, and worthwhile. They are priced so that acquiring an entire library of them is affordable. And they are beginning readers with an important difference—they're written on four levels.

**Step 1 Books,** with their very large type and extremely simple vocabulary, have been created for the very youngest readers. **Step 2 Books** are both longer and slightly more difficult. **Step 3 Books,** written to mid-second-grade reading levels, are for the child who has acquired even greater reading skills. **Step 4 Books** offer exciting nonfiction for the increasingly proficient reader.

Children develop at different ages. **Step into Reading Books,** with their four levels of reading, are designed to help children become good—and interested—readers *faster*. The grade levels assigned to the four steps—preschool through grade 1 for Step 1, grades 1 through 3 for Step 2, grades 2 and 3 for Step 3, and grades 2 through 4 for Step 4—are intended only as guides. Some children move through all four steps very rapidly; others climb the steps over a period of several years. These books will help your child "step into reading" in style!

*For Walker Boyd*

Did you know that your father,
Before you were around,
Used to ride on the subway
Upside down?

E
S

*Library of Congress Cataloging-in-Publication Data:*
Schade, Susan.
Toad eats out / by Susan Schade and Jon Buller.
  p.  cm. — (Step into reading. A Step 1 book)
SUMMARY: Toad's friends have a surprise birthday party for him at his favorite restaurant.
ISBN 0-679-85009-0 (trade) — ISBN 0-679-95009-5 (lib. bdg.)
[1. Restaurants—Fiction.  2. Birthdays—Fiction.  3. Animals—Fiction.
4. Stories in rhyme.]  I. Buller, Jon ill.  II. Title.  III. Series: Step into reading. Step 1 book.
PZ8.3.S287Tm  1995  [E]—dc20  94-5285

Manufactured in the United States of America  10 9 8 7 6 5 4 3 2 1

STEP INTO READING is a trademark of Random House, Inc.

13357

4/96

Step into Reading

# TOAD EATS OUT

A Step 1 Book

By Susan Schade and Jon Buller

Random House 🏠 New York

It's my birthday!

I can do what I want.

I want to eat

in a restaurant!

I pick up Bug.

We drive around.

The rides are fun
at FOOD PLAYGROUND.

They have good fries
at HOT DOG POWER.

We like the clown

at PANCAKE TOWER.

Where do we go?

Where we always do!

Our favorite place,

the CHEW AND VIEW!

# We're hungry now!

# What luck! A spot!

Here we come,

ready or not!

A table for Toad,
right this way.
Bee will be
your server today.

Hey! Cat is here,

and all the guys.

I am amazed!

They shout...

We all put on
our birthday caps.

We spread our napkins
in our laps.

The menu here

is very big.

What are you

having, Pig?

# What's Jumbo Gumbo à la Pat?

# I don't know.
# I'll try that!

Bee writes it down
in a little book.

He goes away
to tell the cook.

Rolls and butter,
water with ice,

plenty of forks—
this place is nice!

Here it comes!
Our food is ready.
Jumbo Gumbo
and spaghetti!

Hot buttered corn
and black-eyed peas.
Would you like
some grated cheese?
Yes, thank you.
And pepper, please.

I take a bite.

Mmm…yum, yum,
yummy!

I eat and eat.

I fill my tummy.

A cake for me!

And candles, too.

And now…let's see
what's in that box.
A big balloon
and matching socks!
A book! A glove!
A model ship!

We're done. We pay.

We leave a tip.

We love to eat out.

We never say no.

Anytime, anyplace,

we're ready to go!